COOKBOOK

Recipes for a Healthy Lifestyle

Mark Ellman

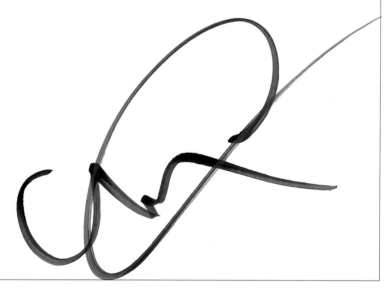

ISBN-13: 978-0-9800241-0-4
ISBN-10: 0-9800241-0-2

Library of Congress Control Number: 2007937332

Printed in the United States of America

Mala Ocean Tavern
1307 Front Street
Lahaina Hawaii 96761
808 667-9394 Phone

Mala Wailea
Wailea Marriott Resort & Spa
3700 Wailea Alanui
Wailea, Maui, Hawaii 96753
808 875-9394

www.malaoceantavern.com

CONTENTS

FOREWORD

Chef and Owner Mark Ellman and his wife Judy have lived on Maui for twenty-two years where they have raised a family of three daughters, Tina, Ariana and Michelle. They have also raised a family of restaurants on three islands in Hawaii: Maui Tacos, Penne Pasta Café and Mala Ocean Tavern. Mark and Judy met over thirty years ago in Calabasas, California, where Judy was the bartender and Mark was a cook in the kitchen at a Mexican restaurant. They fell in love and opened their first restaurant in Sherman Oaks, California, called Cuisine Cuisine, a small Italian eatery. There, they made homemade pasta and great friends.

Long story short, they moved to Colorado for new surroundings, but it was too cold. So in 1985, they moved to Maui and knew they were home.

In 1987, they opened their highly acclaimed Avalon Restaurant and Bar in downtown Lahaina where Mark forged a path of Pacific Rim Cuisine and eventually, along with the following eleven other Hawaii chefs, formed the Hawaii Regional Cuisine movement:

Sam Choy
Roger Dikon
Amy Ferguson Ota
Beverly Gannon
Jean Marie Josselin
George Mavro
Peter Merriman
Phillipe Padovanni
Gary Strehl
Alan Wong
Roy Yamaguchi

Together they published a compilation of recipes, *New Cuisine of Hawaii*, featuring the 12 chefs of Hawaii regional cuisine and giving each chef their own chapter.

Mark and Judy sold Avalon in 1998 to concentrate on their small taco stands called Maui Tacos, which they started in 1993, because they missed their beloved Los Angeles Mexican food. Today, they have nine Maui Tacos in Hawaii on three islands serving authentic Maui-Mex with nothing costing over

$8.95. In 2001, they also opened a small Italian café called Penne Pasta Café where Mark enjoys his Italian heritage with foods from the south of the boot. It is a small family eatery serving paper-thin pizzas, pastas and salads, lamb osso bucco, roast chicken and fresh island fish. Penne Pasta Café is now in its sixth year. And in 2004, Mark and Judy opened Mala Ocean Tavern, a small oceanside tavern serving Mediterranean, Pacific Rim and even some Latino dishes.

Today, Mala is a busy little place feeding locals and tourists lunch, brunch and dinner seven days a week. The locals and tourists would not have it any other way.

In the following pages, you will find recipes that we use at Mala. They are simple, using fresh ingredients and what I like to call "fun flavors"—easy to make at home and food that contributes to a healthy lifestyle.

At Mala, we have a credo we put on the back of our employees' shirts for all customers to see. It simply says, "Practice Aloha." Practicing Aloha is something I need to remind myself to do everyday. It is healthier for one's mind, spirit, attitude and physical being. There is a little bit of Aloha in all of our recipes. It just makes life better. So wherever you are, you too can feel like you live in Hawaii if you Practice Aloha.

Our mission statement

A NOTE FROM MARK AND JUDY

We have always hired good people, and those who work for us at Maui Tacos, Penne Pasta Café and Mala Ocean Tavern are no different. Mala Ocean Tavern is successful because of the team of Pepe and Sergio, partners who also run Maui Tacos and Penne Pasta Café. There are two other "rock stars" who are paramount to the success of Mala Ocean Tavern: General Manager Lisa Chappel and Executive Chef Gregory Denton. Lisa is not only savvy but also nice—the queen of the castle, who runs a tight ship—and there is not anyone who is not charmed by Miss Lisa. Then, there is Chef Gregory. A serious guy with a heart of gold—he is a master at the stove. He is a crown genius when it comes to soups, sauces and new ideas. He is young and has the eye of the tiger. We will have to build him his own place one day where he can soar.

We are all very happy making great, organic, healthy, fresh and delicious food.

We sit in a spot called Mala Wharf, once a great pier where sailors during World War II used to come ashore and enjoy the whaling town of Lahaina. Mala means "garden" in Hawaiian and it truly is a beautiful spot where you sit at the water's edge and gaze upon the islands of Lanai and Molokai and watch the turtles surf while they graze on ogo.

This is the spot of all spots on the west side of Maui and we could not think of a better name for our little restaurant, than to honor where we are, in Mala—our little bit of heaven on earth.

Please enjoy our stories and recipes for life, drink and foods on our island of Maui.

Mahalo and Aloha.

Mark and Judy Ellman

MALA PREP LIST

This is a prep list we use for Mala. The chef will mark what items and how much need to be prepared for the day, every day. It is then divided among the kitchen help.

Each person is given a list and must finish the list before they get to go home. They also have to serve lunch or brunch at the same time.

MIS EN PLACE

Shiitake, Sliced
Onion, Chopped
Garlic, Chopped
Ginger, Chopped
Garlic, Sliced
Chives, Minced
Tomato, Diced
Cilantro, Chopped
Mint, Chopped
Basil, Chopped
Rosemary Garnish
Sage
Parsley, Chopped
Parsley Garnish
Lime Halves
Lemon Wheels
Chile, Chopped
Chinese Black Beans, Rinsed
Preserved Lemon
Mozzarella, Sliced
Arugula
Romaine
Flat Bread
Lavosh
Tortilla Chips
Taro Chips

Mustard
Cheese of the Day
Chickpeas, Cooked
French Fries
Onion Rings
Cucumbers, Cut
Beets, Roasted
Pita Bread, Toasted
Goat Cheese
Fennel, Sliced
Beans, Cooked
Hearts of Palm
Frisée
Olives, Marinated
Celery Sticks
Carrot Sticks
Sugar Snaps
Edamame, Steamed
Corn
Swiss Chard
Artichokes
Ali'i Mushrooms
Ricotta
Feta
Pecorino

Sauces and Salad

Soup of the Day
Egg Salad
Cocktail Sauce
Salsa
Spicy Thai Sauce
Salsa Verde
Chipotle Ketchup
Guacamole
Chile Lime Vinaigrette
Lemon Vinaigrette
Blue Vinaigrette
Fennel Vinaigrette
Ginger Vinaigrette
Avocado Vinaigrette
Pizza Sauce
Harissa
Raita
Strained Yogu
Mignonette
Hummus
Babaganoush
Onion Marmalade
Sofrito
Mac Nut Puree
Figs

Meats

Kobe Burger
Salami, Sliced
Jamon, Sliced
Lamb Meatballs
Marinated Steak
Short Ribs

Pork Cheeks
Lamb Osso Bucco
Pork Osso Bucco
Marinated Wings

Seafood

Ceviche of the Day
Calamari
Fish of the Day
Moi
Shrimp
Oysters
Cooked Shrimp
Clams
Mussels
Sepia
Octopus
Ahi Sashimi

Desserts

Caramel Sauce
Fruit for Miranda
Coquitos
Chocolate Torte
Mac Nut Brittle
Coconut Panna Cotta
Mascarpone
Churros
Chocolate Sauce
Fresh Pineapple Boats
Cookies
Dates
Espresso Mousse

MALA BASICS

AN OCEAN TAVERN

AHI BURGERS

1 pound	fresh **ahi** diced very small
1/4 cup	minced **Maui onion**
2 cloves	chopped fresh **garlic**
1 tablespoon	chopped **piquillo pepper**
1 tablespoon	**Mojo Verde**
1	**egg**
1 teaspoon	ground **cumin**
3 tablespoons	chopped **parsley**
1 teaspoon	**lemon zest**
1/8 cup	**extra virgin olive oil**
1/4 cup	**bread crumbs**
	salt and **pepper**

Mix above well with spoon or hands so as not to squeeze the fish too much.You want to keep it as light and fluffy as possible.It is best to use a chilled stainless steel bowl.

Make 5 ounce patties and chill for at least two hours, or individually wrap them in Saran Wrap and freeze.

To serve: Cook burgers on a flat top griddle or charbroiler or a well greased with olive oil sauté pan for about three minutes on each side or until cooked through. Serve as a sandwich or with one of your favorite salads.

AN OCEAN TAVERN

Mala's Hoisin Glaze

2 C Hoisin Glaze
1/4 C Sweet Soy Sauce
1/4 C Finely Chopped Fresh Ginger
1 Tbsp Minced Fresh Garlic
1 Tsp Sambal Chili Paste
1/4 C Soy Sauce
1/4 C Fresh Orange Juice
1/2 C Rice Wine Vinegar

Combine all the ingredients and mix well.
You can adjust the amount of Sambal if
you prefer a spicy version.
All ingredients should be available in
the Asian aisle of your local supermarket
or at any Asian grocery store.
Makes a great all purpose sauce
that can be used with any protein or tofu.

ALI'I MUSHROOMS

These mushrooms are grown in Hamakua on the Big Island, by two wonderful folks who have a love for fungus. Please visit their website, www.hhfhawaii.com.

The mushrooms are good on their own or on top of a pizza, salad or steak—very similar to the texture of a Porcini.

4 ounces	sliced **Ali'i mushrooms**

Toss with

1 ounce	**olive oil**
2 cloves	sliced **garlic**

In a sauté pan add 2 ounces olive oil over high heat. Add mushrooms and cook until brown. Add

2 ounces	**garlic oil sauce**

Toss and add

1 tablespoon	chopped **parsley**

Season with salt and pepper. Serve with wedge of lemon.

AN OCEAN TAVERN

GARLIC OIL SAUCE

1/2 cup   freshly chopped **garlic**
1 cup   pure **olive oil**

Over a very low flame place garlic and oil and salt in sauté pan and cook very slowly for about 45 minutes until garlic turns a nice light brown. Remove from heat and cool. When cool add

1/4 cup   fresh chopped **parsley**

Stir and chill.

AN OCEAN TAVERN

SERGIO'S ANCHO STEAK SAUCE

5 cloves	fresh **garlic**
5	fresh **tomatoes** quartered
5	**pasilla peppers**
2	**ancho chile peppers**
2	**guajillo peppers**
1	whole peeled **onion** quartered
4	whole **cloves**
2 tablespoons	whole **oregano**
2	**bay leaves**
1/2 cook's spoon	**rosemary**
1 quart	**water**
1/2 cup	**apple sauce**
	salt and **pepper** to taste

Puree all the ingredients for one minute and bring to a boil. Simmer for 30 minutes or until thick. Add salt and pepper to taste.

This recipe was created for Mala by Chef Sergio Perez. You can taste Sergio's roots of Mexico City in every bite.

It is a great sauce with any meat. We use it on our Prime Flat Iron Steak. It is also good with Lamb Chops.

AN OCEAN TAVERN

JUDY'S AVOCADO VINAIGRETTE

1	fresh ripe **avocado**
1/8 cup	fresh **lemon juice**
1 tablespoon	**white vinegar**
1/2 cup	**extra virgin olive oil**
1/2 teaspoon	fresh **lemon zest**
1 teaspoon	fresh minced **garlic**
1 tablespoon	fresh chopped **parsley**
	salt and **pepper** to taste

Mash the avocado with a whisk in a mixing bowl. Mix in the rest of the ingredients. Add salt and pepper to taste.

Let sit for 30 minutes to have the flavors blend. You also could add one of your favorite fresh herbs as well.

This is one of those dressings my wife Judy came up with to serve at home with a bowl full of veggies and Heirloom Tomatoes. This dressing screams Summer.

BALINESE MARINADE FOR LAMB AND STEAK

1/2 cup	**sweet kecap manis** (palm sugar soy sauce from Bali)
2 tablespoons	fresh chopped **ginger**
2 tablespoons	fresh chopped **garlic**
2 tablespoons	fresh chopped **mint**
1/4 cup	coarse grain **mustard**
2 teaspoons	**sambal**

Mix all the ingredients in a bowl and marinade your favorite lamb or steak for at least 6 hours. Barbecue over a medium fire.

Be careful not to burn the marinade because the palm sugar has a tendency to cook very quickly.

This is particularly great with Lamb Chops. I fell in love with Kecap Manis and had to go to Bali to see how the Balinese used this beautiful sauce. The flavor right out of the bottle is quite different and not as good as when it is heated and caramelized. It has a very seductive flavor.

AN OCEAN TAVERN

BALSAMIC ROASTED EGGPLANT

2	large **eggplants**
1/2 cup	aged **balsamic vinegar**
3/4 cup	**extra virgin olive oil**
	kosher or **sea salt** to taste
	fresh **cracked black pepper** to taste

Heat oven to 425 degrees. Wash eggplant and using a peeler, peel three strips from the eggplant, equal distance from each other. Slice eggplant into 1/2-inch slices.

In a large bowl, combine balsamic vinegar, salt and pepper. Mix and taste. The mixture should be strong in flavor. Add the olive oil and mix well. Add all the eggplant slices and mix well. When the eggplant has soaked up most of the liquid, place them on a sheet pan. They can slightly overlap each other. Pour any excess liquid evenly over the eggplant. Place in a preheated oven for 8 minutes.

Open oven and rotate if you notice uneven cooking. Cook for another 5 minutes. The eggplant should be dark, not burnt and should be very soft. Remove from sheet pan and serve or cool and store for later.

This is excellent as a side vegetable or served on a crusty French bread.

AN OCEAN TAVERN

SALAD OF BEETS WITH FENNEL VINAIGRETTE AND WARM GOAT CHEESE

2 pounds	**beets**, quartered
	olive oil to coat
4 cloves	chopped **garlic**
1	**bay leaf**
1 teaspoon	**fennel seeds**
1 teaspoon	chopped **ginger**
1 teaspoon	**peppercorns**, crushed
Dressing:	
1	**Maui onion**
1/2 cup	**red wine vinegar**
1 tablespoon	crushed **anise seeds**
1 teaspoon	**ground pepper**
1 teaspoon	**sugar**
2 tablespoons	fresh chopped **fennel leaves**
1 cup	**olive oil**

Heat oven to 375 degrees. Combine beets with olive oil to coat. Add the garlic, bay leaf, fennel seeds, ginger and peppercorns. Roast in oven until tender, about 40 minutes. Cool the beets and skin.

For the dressing, dice the onion and salt it for ten minutes. Whisk in red wine vinegar.

Add the beets to the vinaigrette and serve on top of a small amount of greens and thinly sliced fennel bulb with an herb oil.

On top of the beets, place 2 pieces of soft goat cheese rolled in panko flakes and bake or fry until golden.

AN OCEAN TAVERN

BRAISED KALE

1/2 ounce	**olive oil**
1/2 ounce	**clarified butter**
1 teaspoon	chopped **onion**
1 teaspoon	sliced **garlic**
	salt and **pepper** to taste
4 ounces	rough chopped **kale**
3 ounces	**San Marzano tomatoes**, canned
2 ounces	**white wine**
	grated **pecorino cheese**

Heat oven to 400 degrees. In a pan, add olive oil and clarified butter. Add chopped onion, sliced garlic, salt and pepper to taste and cook for 30 seconds.

Add kale, San Marzano tomatoes and white wine. Cover and cook until it boils. Place the mixture in an ovenproof plate and top with grated pecorino cheese. Cook in the oven until it browns—about 10 minutes. Serve immediately.

Kale is one of those great vegetables that is wonderful raw in a salad, quickly stir-fried in an Asian preparation, or slowly braised with tomatoes and garlic. Very versatile. This recipe is especially good with canned San Marzano Tomatoes from southern Italy. The tomatoes are naturally sweet and add great flavor.

AN OCEAN TAVERN

CARROT BUTTERNUT CORIANDER SOUP

2 pounds	**butternut squash** with cooked skins and seeds removed

Place 1/2 cup of **olive oil** in a soup pot and add

1/2	chopped **Maui onion**
1 teaspoon	**paprika**
1 teaspoon	ground **cumin**
1 teaspoon	**tumeric**
2 teaspoons	ground **coriander**
2 teaspoons	**salt**
1 teaspoon	**pepper**

Sauté for 10 minutes, then add

	squash pulp
5	**carrots** peeled and chopped
2 teaspoons	**sugar**

Cook for 10 minutes then add

5 cups	**chicken stock**
2 cups	**water**

Bring to a boil and simmer for 40 minutes. Puree soup until very smooth. Season to taste. Garnish with fresh chopped cilantro and 1 teaspoon yogurt.

AN OCEAN TAVERN

BUTTERNUT PUMPKIN AND GINGER SOUP

2 pounds	cooked **butternut squash** pulp
4 tablespoons	fresh chopped **ginger**
2	chopped **Maui onions**
5	fresh chopped **garlic cloves**
2	chopped **carrots**
4	chopped **celery stalks**
4 tablespoons	fresh chopped **basil**
4 tablespoons	fresh chopped **parsley**
2 teaspoons	**fennel seeds**
1 teaspoon	**cumin seeds**
1 clove	**cardamon**
1 pinch	**nutmeg**
1 bottle	**white wine**
1 quart	**heavy cream**
1 cup	**coconut milk**
2	**bay leaves**
2	**kaffir lime leaves**

Place all the ingredients except for the parsley in a pot with 2 cups of water and bring to a soft boil. Simmer for 45 minutes.

Puree until smooth, strain and add cornstarch slurry. Cook for 5 minutes more and add salt and pepper to taste. Serve with a sprinkle of parsley.

AN OCEAN TAVERN

MALA CAESAR DRESSING

1	**egg yolk**
2 tablespoons	coarse grain **mustard**
5 tablespoons	fresh chopped **tarragon**, divided
4	finely chopped **garlic cloves**
2 ounces	ground **parmesan**
1 tablespoon	coarse ground **pepper**
	juice of 2 **lemons**
6	whole **anchovy filets**
2 cups	**extra virgin olive oil**
2 tablespoons	**red wine vinegar**
	salt and **pepper** to taste

Place egg yolk, mustard, 4 tablespoons of tarragon, garlic, parmesan, pepper, lemon juice and anchovy filets in a Cuisinart and pulse until smooth.

Continue to puree and in a slow steady stream add extra virgin olive oil until dressing becomes thick. Add red wine vinegar and fold in 1 tablespoon of tarragon. Add salt and pepper to taste.

For salad, have cleaned romaine leaves chilled and dry. Grated parmesan is essential to help the dressing stick to the leaves, so sprinkle liberally. Then add some dressing—just enough to coat the leaves. You can add croutons or, like we do at Mala, Grilled Flax seed toast and white anchovies.

AN OCEAN TAVERN

CARAMEL MIRANDA™

1-2/3 cups	**sugar**
1/2 cup	**water**
1 teaspoon	**cream of tartar**
1 cup	**heavy whipping cream**
1 teaspoon	**unsalted butter**
20 ounces	**dark chocolate chips**
1/4 cup	**baby coconuts**, cut in half
1/4 cup	diced **Maui pineapple**
1/4 cup	**star fruit**, sliced into stars
1/4 cup	diced **apple bananas**
1/4 cup	diced **Maui mango**
1/4 cup	**papaya**
6 ounces	**Häagen-Dazs Macadamia Brittle ice cream**

In a heavy saucepan, add water, sugar and cream of tartar. Mix well until sugar dissolves. Heat over medium heat until mixture turns a dark amber color. Remove from heat and stir cream in and mix well with a whisk.

Set aside and add butter, stir.

Ladle 6 ounces of caramel on an ovenproof plate and sprinkle the fruit and chocolate chips on top of the sauce. Place under the broiler until fruit is hot and caramelized.

Spoon 6 ounces of Häagen-Dazs Macadamia Brittle ice cream in center of hot plate and serve.

At Avalon, Caramel Miranda was essentially the only dessert served. Today, it definitely is the most popular at Mala Ocean Tavern.

AN OCEAN TAVERN

CEVICHE DE CALAMAR/CALAMARI CEVICHE

All of the Ceviches Tiraditos and salsas in this section are by Chef Jose Pepe Vega

12	small **calamari**, cleaned and cut 1/2 inch body on
1	clove fresh **garlic**
1/2	**serrano chile**
2	**lemons**, juiced
2	**limes**, juiced
1/2	**red onion**
1	**tomato**
1	**fire-roasted red pepper**
	freshly ground **black pepper** to taste
	parsley for garnish
	sliced **green olives** for garnish

Submerge the calamari in 2 gallons of boiling water for 10 seconds. Pull out and place the calamari in a bowl and chill.

In a blender, add garlic, serrano chile, juice of 2 limes and 2 lemons and blend. Pour over calamari, season with black pepper and let it rest for 10 minutes.

On a serving platter, julienne onion and tomato over the calamari, fire-roasted red pepper and parsley. Mix all and garnish with a slice of lime and olives.

TIRADITO DE OPAKAPAKA

10 ounces   fresh **opakapaka**
5   **limes**, juiced
1/2   fresh **garlic clove**
pinch   **white pepper**
pinch   **salt**
1/2   **jalapeño** or **aji (Peruvian hot pepper)**
   tomato
   cilantro
   chopped **parsley**
   salt
   olive oil

Slice the opakapaka very thin. In a bowl, combine the lime juice, garlic, white pepper, salt and jalapeño (or aji). Pour over fish.

Mix tomato, cilantro, parsley and salt. Garnish each piece of fish with this mixture.

Add a final touch of olive oil.

AN OCEAN TAVERN

CEVICHE DE CAMARON (AGUA CHILE)

12	large **shrimp**
10	**limes**, juiced
1/2	fresh **jalapeño**
3	**cilantro stems**
	salt and **pepper** to taste
	red onion
	avocado, sliced
	olive oil
	piquillo peppers, sliced

Cut the shrimp in half and place on a platter. Combine the lime juice, jalapeño, cilantro stems and salt and pepper to taste. Let it rest for 15 minutes.

Garnish the shrimp with red onion and avocado slices. Then add dressing, olive oil and slices of piquillo peppers.

Serve with sliced tomatoes or pico de gallo and baked chips.

AN OCEAN TAVERN

OYSTER CEVICHE

fresh **oysters** in shell open in half
fresh **tomatillo**
cilantro salsa
lime, juiced
olive oil

In a bowl, combine tomatillo, cilantro salsa, lime juice and olive oil.
Pour evenly over the oysters.

TOMATILLO SALSA

15	fresh **tomatillo**s, diced
3 teaspoons	chopped **cilantro**
1	chopped **serrano chile**
3 teaspoons	**Maui onion**
1 teaspoon	**olive oil**
1 to 2 teaspoons	**soy sauce**

Caramelize the Maui onion in the olive oil. In a bowl combine the
caramelized Maui onion, tomatillos, chopped cilantro, serrano chile and
soy sauce (add 1 or 2 teaspoons depending on the saltiness).

AN OCEAN TAVERN

KONA LOBSTER CEVICHE

3	whole **lobsters**
2	**limes**, juiced
1/2	**red onion**
2 tablespoons	**olive oil**
3 tablespoons	**cilantro**, chopped
2 tablespoons	**soy sauce**
1/2	**orange**, juiced
1/2	**lemon**, juiced
1	**yellow tomato**, diced
2	**bay leaves**
1	**beer (Corona)**

Fill a pot with water to cover the lobsters. Bring to a boil. Add bay leaves, beer and juice from the orange. Boil the lobsters until they start turning pink-red. Pull out the lobsters and cool in ice water.

Cut each lobster in pieces. Add lime juice, lemon juice, soy sauce and olive oil. Marinate for 10 minutes, then add red onion, diced tomato and cilantro.

If you like a little heat, add Maui Tacos Chipotle Pineapple Salsa. Mix well and serve on a bed of greens. Garnish with baked (not fried) tortilla chips.

AN OCEAN TAVERN

CHERMOULA MARINADE FOR
FISH, CHICKEN OR STEAK

3 teaspoons	ground **cumin**
3 teaspoons	**sweet paprika**
1 teaspoon	ground **turmeric**
1/2 teaspoon	**cayenne pepper**
2	fresh **garlic cloves**, minced
1/2 cup	grated **Maui onion**
1 teaspoon	**salt**
	fresh **ground pepper**
1/2 cup	fresh chopped **parsley**
1/2 cup	fresh chopped **cilantro**
1/2 cup	fresh **lemon juice**
1/2 cup	**extra virgin olive oil**
1/4 cup	**water**

Combine all the ingredients in a food processor or blender. Blend until smooth.

This is a North African marinade that adds a bold delightful flavor. Marinate up to 24 hours.

CHERRY TOMATO VINAIGRETTE

1 cup	**extra virgin olive oil**
1/4 cup	**balsamic vinegar**
5	minced fresh **garlic cloves**
	salt and **pepper** to taste
1 pint	**cherry** or **grape tomatoes**, cut in halves or quarters
8	fresh **basil leaves**, minced
1 tablespoon	fresh chopped **parsley**
pinch	dried **red chili pepper**

In a bowl, whisk all the ingredients together. Leave at room temperature. Serve with Fresh Grilled Fish or Chicken.

CHICKPEAS

3 cups	dried **chickpeas (garbanzo beans)**
2 tablespoons	**salt**

Cover chickpeas with water and soak overnight.

Drain and cover with water 2 inches over the chickpeas. Simmer uncovered until the skins begin to crack and the chickpeas are tender—about 1-1/4 hours. Add salt. Cool in its liquid and leave chilled until ready to use but should be used within three days at the most.

Use these to make hummus, soup or salad.

CHICKEN STOCK

3 pounds	**chicken parts**, remove excess fat
1 gallon	**water** (or enough water to cover the bones and vegetables by 2 inches)
1	large **onion**, quartered
3	**carrots**, peeled and diced
4	stalks of **celery**, diced
6	**parsley stems**
1 tablespoon	**dried thyme**
2	**bay leaves**

Bring all the ingredients to a boil and simmer for 3 hours. Strain and discard the bones and vegetables. Place in the refrigerator.

AN OCEAN TAVERN

CHICKEN TIKKA KEBAB

1 pound	**chicken breast**, boneless and skinless
	salt to taste
1 teaspoon	**chili powder**
1 teaspoon	**coriander seeds**, ground
1/8 cup	**lime juice**
1	**garlic clove**, minced
1 tablespoon	grated fresh **ginger**
1/4 cup	fresh chopped **cilantro**
2 tablespoons	**olive oil**
1/2 cup	**yogurt**
	lime slices to garnish

Rinse chicken and pat dry with paper towels. Cut into 3/4 inch cubes. Thread onto short skewers. Put skewered chicken into a shallow nonmetal dish.

In a small bowl, mix together yogurt, ginger root, garlic, chili powder, coriander, cilantro, salt, lime juice and oil. Pour over skewered chicken and turn to coat completely in marinade. Cover and refrigerate 6 hours or overnight to allow chicken to absorb the flavors.

Heat grill. Place skewered chicken on grill rack and cook 5 to 7 minutes, turning skewers and basting occasionally with any remaining marinade. Serve hot and garnish with lime slices.

AN OCEAN TAVERN

CHICKEN WING MARINADE

1/4 cup	**pomegranate syrup**
1/4 cup	**kecap manis**
2 tablespoons	fresh chopped **ginger**
2 tablespoons	coarse grain **mustard**
1 tablespoon	**sambal**
1/8 cup	fresh chopped **mint**
1/4 cup	**tamarind paste**
2 teaspoons	**ras el hanout** (Moroccan spice mix)

Heat oven to 375 degrees. In a bowl, mix all the ingredients and set aside.

Cook chicken wings in the oven with olive oil and salt and pepper until cooked through.

Toss the wings in the sauce and fry until crispy. Sprinkle with minced green onions and toasted sesame seeds.

AN OCEAN TAVERN

CHILLED CUCUMBER MINT SOUP

2	large **English cucumbers**, peeled, deseeded
2 cups	**water**
1/2 cup	**sour cream**
1/4 cup	**sugar**
1 tablespoon	**salt**
1/4 cup	fresh **mint**, leaves only
1/2 cup	**extra virgin olive oil**
1	**mint sprig**

Combine the cucumber and water in a blender. Puree mixture until smooth. Add sugar, salt, sour cream and fresh mint. Continue to puree until all ingredients are completely incorporated. While blender is still on, slowly add the olive oil. Strain through a fine strainer. Store in refrigerator for at least 1 hour before serving.

Serve with diced cucumber, mint sprig and olive oil. Use as a sauce—it is great with grilled fish.

AN OCEAN TAVERN

CHOCOLATE TORTE SOUFFLÉ (Flourless)

1/2 pound	**dark chocolate**
1/4 pound	**unsalted butter**
5	**eggs**
5 ounces	**sugar**

Heat oven to 300 degrees. In a bain-marie, melt chocolate and butter.

Meanwhile, separate eggs. Add sugar to the yolks and mix for at least 60 seconds until sugar is dissolved and mixture is ribbonlike. Beat egg whites until soft peaks.

Butter a 10 x 2-inch round cake pan heavily so the cake will not stick and place it in the freezer for 15 minutes. Butter it again and place it back in the freezer.

Mix the chocolate mixture with the yolk mixture. Fold in egg whites gently.

Remove pan from freezer and place the mixture into the pan. Cook in oven for 1 hour and 10 minutes. Remove from oven and cool for 15 minutes at room temperature. Invert cake onto a plate and serve with fresh whipped cream, chocolate shavings and ground espresso.

I learned this simple recipe from a great pastry chef, Claude Koberle at the Ma Maison Restaurant in Los Angeles in the late '70s. It is a time-less recipe.

AN OCEAN TAVERN

COCONUT PANNA COTTA

1 ounce	**gelatin**
4 cups	**milk**
1/2 cup	**sugar**
1/2 teaspoon	**salt**
27 ounces	**coconut milk**

Sprinkle the gelatin on top of the milk and let sit for 10 minutes. Add sugar and salt and heat to a simmer. Add coconut milk and then strain into oiled molds.

Chill overnight and serve.

To serve you may have to place bottom of mold in warm water for a few seconds to invert.

It is great with fresh fruit like raspberries or a lillikoi sauce.

Panna Cotta is one of the simplest recipes with so many variations.

AN OCEAN TAVERN

BRAISED OCTOPUS

1	**octopus**
1/2 cup	**olive oil**
1	**bay leaf**
2	**garlic cloves**
1	**onion**, diced
1	**lemon**, juiced
1	**orange**, juiced

Wash octopus. Cut it below the eyes and head and remove its beak. In a heavy pot, combine octopus, olive oil, bay leaf, garlic cloves and onion. Add the juice from the lemon and the orange and place the squeezed lemon and orange in the pot as well.

Cover and cook slowly for 40 to 50 minutes or until octopus has exuded its own juices and turns deep pink and tender. Remove octopus and cool.

In Hawaii, the locals call octopus "squid." I have no idea why.

CREAM OF ALI'I MUSHROOM SOUP

1/4 pound	**butter**
1/4 cup	**extra virgin olive oil**
4	**garlic cloves**
1/4 teaspoon	**crushed red pepper**
1	**white onion**, chopped
1/2	**red onion**, chopped
1 pound	**ali'i mushrooms**, sliced (can substitute with **button mushrooms)**
1/4 cup	**all-purpose flour**
1/2 cup	**white wine**
3/4 quart	**low-sodium chicken broth** or **water**
1/2 quart	**heavy cream**
	kosher salt and **black pepper**

Melt butter with olive oil in a heavy-bottom saucepan over medium-high heat. Add garlic and crushed red pepper. Cook until garlic starts to brown. Add red and white onions and cook until soft, about 6 to 7 minutes. Add mushrooms and cook for 6 to 7 minutes.

Sprinkle flour over the mushrooms and onions, stirring constantly. It is okay for the flour to stick to the bottom of the pan, but, before it burns, add the white wine and continue to stir. It is very important to stir continuously throughout this process. Wooden spoons are the best for making soup.

Cook this for 1 to 2 minutes then add your broth or water and the heavy cream. Continue to stir continuously until it comes to a boil.

Continued on next page

AN OCEAN TAVERN

Reduce heat to low. Continue to stir occasionally and simmer for 10 minutes. Remove from stove. Puree in blender. *Note:* If soup is still hot when blending, then only fill the container half way.

Cover with lid and drape a kitchen towel over the top and start at a low speed and gradually turn up the speed. Puree for about 1 minute. Pour in pot or storage container and add salt and pepper to taste. Serve really hot.

Feel free to add any fresh herbs at this point. Get fancy and add truffle oil. Not too much or it will overtake the ali'i mushroom flavor. Good food takes time and patience.

CREAM OF OLOWALU TOMATO SOUP

1/4 pound	**unsalted butter**
1/4 cup	**extra virgin olive oil**
7	**garlic cloves**, whole, peeled, stems removed
1/2	small **jalapeño**, diced (keep seeds for more spice)
1	small **yellow onion**, diced
1/2	small **red onion**, diced
3 or 4	medium **red Olowalu tomatoes**, diced
3 or 4	medium **yellow Olowalu tomatoes**, diced
2 teaspoons	**kosher salt** or **sea salt**
1 pint	**heavy cream**
1 cup	**water**
	fresh **cracked black pepper** as needed
6	thinly sliced **basil leaves**

1/4 cup   **mascarpone cheese**
                extra virgin olive oil as needed
                lavosh, **crackers** or your favorite **bread**

Heat butter and oil in pot. Add garlic cloves and jalapeño. Cook and stir with wooden spoon until butter and garlic start to brown. Always use wooden spoons when making soups. It helps release the fond (the brown stuff at the bottom of the pot) without scratching the pot and releasing any off flavors.

Reduce heat and add onions to pot. Cook until onions are soft and translucent. Core and cut tomatoes. Add tomatoes and salt to onions. Stir the tomatoes very well to distribute the salt. The salt will help release the natural water in the tomatoes. Continue to stir until the liquid starts to reduce. Reduce until liquid is half of its original volume. This will concentrate the flavor of the tomato a great deal.

Turn heat off under soup. Add cream slowly while stirring. Add salt and pepper to taste. Turn heat back on to medium. Bring to boil. Turn off and puree in blender. To prevent burns, fill blender only half way. Put cover on but remove plastic piece on the top part of the blender. Then cover with a towel. Start on low and increase speed gradually. This will decrease the escape of hot steam.

Strain soup through fine strainer into storage container or different pot. Add more water to soup until desired texture is achieved. Although this soup is very good the same day, it (like all soups) is also better the next day. Always taste for seasoning.

Reheat soup while stirring until it boils. Turn off and portion into serving bowls. Add mascarpone cheese, oil and serve cracker on the side. Add sliced basil. Enjoy!

AN OCEAN TAVERN

DATES WITH MASCARPONE

dried Medjool dates
mascarpone cheese

Split dates and seed. Place a small scoop of mascarpone cheese inside each date. Refrigerate for at least 1 hour. Serve with a small piece of macadamia nut for garnish.

EDAMAME PUREE

We use the edamame along with tomatillo salsa in our molcajete (lava) bowls. I saw it used by Charlie Trotter once and thought it would be a perfect healthy start at Mala instead of the usual bread and butter. The simplicity of the edamame pairs very well with the complex flavors of the tomatillo salsa. Use tortilla chips for dipping.

1 pound	steamed **edamame beans** fresh or frozen
1 cup	**extra virgin olive oil**
1/2 cup	**rice wine vinegar**
	salt and **pepper** to taste

In a food processor, place edamame beans and puree slowly. Add olive oil until mixture is smooth and creamy. Add rice wine vinegar and salt and pepper to taste. Add a little water (if necessary) if mixture is too thick.

FARRO SALAD

I love this salad because the farro is nutty and chewy.

1 cup	**farro Ancient Wheat from Italy**
3 cups	**water**
1 cup	**extra virgin olive oil**
2 teaspoons	**red wine vinegar**
1 cup	**grape tomatoes**, cut in half
1/4 cup	**cucumber**, peeled, seeded and diced same size as tomatoes
1/4 cup	**pecorino cheese**, diced small
1/4 cup	**basil leaves**, torn by hand
	salt and **pepper** to taste

Combine farro, water, and salt and cook uncovered at a simmer until tender—about 20 to 30 minutes. Drain and spread on a sheet pan to cool quickly.

Whisk together olive oil, red wine vinegar, salt and pepper.

Combine the cool farro with tomatoes, cucumber, pecorino cheese and basil leaves.

To serve, mix 4 ounces of farro with 2 tablespoons of vinaigrette or just enough to coat. Garnish with 1 basil leaf.

AN OCEAN TAVERN

FRESH AKULE OVEN ROASTED WITH LEMON, GARLIC AND PARSLEY

4	**akule filets**, **boned**
3 tablespoons	**extra virgin olive oil**
	fresh chopped **garlic**
1/4 cup	diced **tomato**
3	sliced **garlic cloves**
3	**olives** Kalamata pitted
1 tablespoon	chopped **parsley**
1	**lemon sliced into rounds**
	salt and **pepper** to taste

Heat oven to 400 degrees. Marinate akule filets with olive oil and fresh chopped garlic. In an ovenproof dish, place tomato, garlic cloves, olives and lemon slices. Sprinkle with 3 tablespoons olive oil. Place filets on top and season with salt and pepper.

Place in the preheated oven for 10 minutes or until cooked through. Remove and sprinkle with fresh chopped parsley. If possible serve it in the dish it was cooked in. Serve with a hearty red wine and crusty bread.

Akule is a popular local fish that looks a lot like a sardine or mackerel. You can always find it being sold out of a cooler on the side of the road by the fishermen. Akule is also great raw with extra virgin olive oil, shallots, and lemon.

AN OCEAN TAVERN

FRIED SQUID (CALAMARI)

1 pound	**squid**
1/2 cup	**whole wheat flour**
1/2 cup	**semolina flour**
6	fresh **sage leaves**
2	thin slices of **lemon**
	salt and **pepper** to taste

Clean, slice, rinse and dry squid. Keep chilled. Place squid in seasoned whole wheat flour mixed with semolina flour, salt and pepper. Toss in sage leaves and lemon. Fry squid, leaves, and lemon in 350 degrees oil until golden brown. Remove and dry on paper towel.

Serve with lemon wedges and Aioli.

GARLIC SPINACH

2 pounds	**spinach**, cleaned
2 gallons	**water**, boiling
1 cup	**kosher** or **sea salt**
1/4 cup	**unsalted butter**
2	**garlic cloves**, minced
1/2 teaspoon	**kosher** or **sea salt**
1 teaspoon	**black pepper**

Add 1 cup of salt to boiling water. Blanch the spinach in four different batches. Add spinach to the boiling water and remove almost immediately. Cool down in an ice and water mixture (a 2:1 ratio of ice to water). Remove from the ice bath as soon as the spinach is cool and squeeze out all the water or as much as you can. Set the spinach aside on a paper towel. Keep in refrigerator until ready to serve.

In a sauté pan, melt butter. Add garlic and cook until butter and garlic start to brown. Add salt and pepper then add the spinach and mix so garlic stops cooking. Cook long enough so that the salt and pepper are totally incorporated. Remove from sauté pan and put on plate or other flat surface so the spinach will stop cooking. Place in refrigerator.

GINGER VINAIGRETTE

This simple but tasty dressing is great for a Chinese chicken salad.

1/2 cup	**sugar**
8	**garlic cloves**, peeled
1/2 cup	peeled **ginger**, chopped
1 cup	**low-salt soy sauce**
1/4 cup	**red wine vinegar**
1 cup	**water**
1 cup	**olive oil**

Place all the ingredients in a blender and puree for 60 seconds. Strain through a fine mesh strainer. Chill.

Mala Ocean Tavern

Michelle and Ariana, daughters
and Managers at Mala

Tio Jose who makes the best Ceviche in the world

Lisa Chappel, Manager Extraordinaire

John and Alex

Ariana and Tennyson

Chella Vega (Pepe's wife), Cindy Beadles (our Office Manager), and Judy Ellman

Magic Islands Chefs

Mala Bar

Chef Greg Denton and Ben Klein
with the Dalai Lama in Maui

Judy, Ben
and Greg
cooking for the
Dalai Lama

Pasta Bolognese for his Holiness

His Holiness holding hands with my wife
Judy

Dalai Lama on Maui; we personally cooked lunch for him two days in a row

Mala Ocean Tavern

Interior of Mala

Mala at night

Hoisin Glazed Baby Back Ribs

Wok Fried Opakapaka Ginger Garlic Black Bean Sauce

Seared Sashimi

Gado Gado Salad

Lamb Pita and Kobe Cheese Burger with Maytag Blue

Filet Mignon with Sesame Pancakes

Mala at night

Mala means "garden" in Hawaiian and it truly is a beautiful spot where you sit at the water's edge and gaze upon the islands of Lanai and Molokai and watch the turtles surf while they graze on ogo.

Mala sunset

Quartet of Hummus, Babaganoush, Greek Feta, Raita and Grilled

Mala Ocean Flatbread with Mahi Mahi and Ono

Hood Canal Oyster Shooters with Ponzu and Wasabi

Roasted Beet Salad Fennel Vinaigrette, with Surfing Goat Cheese

Spicy Pomegranate Chicken Wings

Snake River Farms Kobe Cheeseburger

My Big Fat Greek Salad

Mahi Mahi Ceviche

Ahi Bruschetta

AN OCEAN TAVERN

GRILLED PECORINO AND
MAC NUT SANDWICH

*This is a variation of a sandwich I had at one of my favorite bakeries,
Tartine, in San Francisco.*

2	slices **bread**
	butter
4 ounces	**pecorino cheese**

Nut filling:

1 cup	roasted **macadamia nuts**
1	**garlic clove**
1 teaspoon	chopped **ginger**
1/4 cup	**olive oil**
1 tablespoon	**lemon juice**
1/2 teaspoon	**lemon zest**
1/2 teaspoon	chopped **orange zest**
1 tablespoon	chopped **parsley**
1 teaspoon	**salt**
1/2 teaspoon	ground **black pepper**

Coarsely chop nuts then add rest of nut filling ingredients to a coarse
paste.

Butter the outside of each piece of bread. Spread 1 tablespoon of nut
filling on each side. Add one slice of pecorino cheese. Grill until crusty.
Slice and serve hot.

AN OCEAN TAVERN

HEARTS OF PALM SALAD

Salad:

1	6-inch piece freshly sliced **hearts of palm**, julienned
1	3-inch piece of **carrot**, peeled and julienned
6	**grape tomatoes**, cut in half
1/2 teaspoon	toasted **sesame seeds**
1/2 teaspoon	snipped **chives**
1/2 teaspoon	minced **preserved lemon**
1/2 teaspoon	fresh chopped **ginger**

Dressing:

2 ounces	**extra virgin olive oil**
1 ounce	**champagne vinegar**
1/2 ounce	**sesame oil**
	salt and **pepper** to taste

Place salad ingredients in a bowl and add dressing ingredients. Place mixture on a bed of frisée and mâche. Add a pinch of sumak powder dusted on top.

Fresh hearts of palm were not available in Hawaii 15 years ago. University of Hawaii developed a program with farmers in Hawaii of what palm would serve best. The answer? The peach palm.

AN OCEAN TAVERN

HOISIN GLAZED PORK RIBS

Yum...

2	**pork ribs**, full racks
1/4 cup	**kosher salt** and **sea salt**
1 cup	fresh **ground black pepper**
2 quarts	**non-trans fat frying oil (vegetable oil)**
1 cup	**hoisin glaze** (see recipe)
1 tablespoon	**sesame seeds**, toasted
2 tablespoons	**green onion**, sliced

Heat oven to 350 degrees. Place the ribs on a pan that will fit the whole rack width and length. Season both sides with salt and pepper. Cover with aluminum foil so it is airtight. Place pan of ribs in heated oven for 1-1/2 to 2 hours. Check on them after 1-1/2 hours with a knife. If the knife goes completely through with little resistance, the ribs are done. Remove and cool.

Cut cooled ribs between the bones. Heat frying oil in a large heavy-bottom pot. Fill the pot only 1/2 way to the top. You need plenty of room when deep frying. Using a thermometer, bring the temperature of oil to 350 degrees. Very carefully, using tongs place the ribs one at a time in the fryer. Do this in two or three batches, depending on how large your pot is. Remove ribs when they get brown and crusty on the outside of the rib. This will take 3 to 4 minutes for each batch.

Place them in a bowl and coat them very well with the hoisin glaze. Let them sit for 1 to 2 minutes.

Place the ribs on top of your favorite salad or mashed potatoes. Finish the ribs with green onion and sesame seeds.

AN OCEAN TAVERN

HOMEMADE CHIPOTLE KETCHUP

1 can	**tomatoes**
1/2 cup	**olive oil**
1/2	**Maui onion**, finely chopped
4	**garlic cloves**, minced
2 tablespoons	minced fresh **ginger**
1/4 cup	**brown sugar**
dash	**cloves**
1 teaspoon	**fennel seeds**
	salt and **ground black pepper** to taste
1/4 cup	**chipotle de adobo**
1	**bay leaf**
1	**cinnamon stick**
2 tablespoons	**red wine vinegar**
1/4 cup	**lemon juice**

Heat the oil in a saucepan and sauté the onions until clear. Add the garlic, ginger, sugar, spices, vinegar and lime juice. Add the tomatoes and chipotle. Bring to a boil and simmer for an hour. Puree with an immersion blender. Chill overnight before using.

I use this ketchup sometimes with very thin fried Maui onion rings.

HOOD CANAL OYSTER SHOOTER

4	**Hood Canal oysters** (Washington State)
2 teaspoons	**black tobiko caviar**
2 teaspoons	**wasabi tobiko**
2 ounces	**ponzu sauce (see recipe on page 59)**
pinch	**chives**, finely chopped
pinch	**wasabi paste**

Divide this recipe by four.

Place 1 oyster in a chilled shot glass. Add tobiko caviar and wasabi tobiko. Add ponzu sauce, chopped chives and wasabi paste. Ball the wasabi paste and place it on the lip of the glass so you can manage your own heat level. Place the glass over crushed ice and serve.

LEMON TAHINI VINAIGRETTE

1/4 cup	**Dijon mustard**
1/8 cup	**tahini**
1	**garlic clove**, minced
1 teaspoon	**cracked pepper**
2 ounces	**feta cheese**
1/4 cup	**lemon juice**
1 teaspoon	**Greek oregano**
1 teaspoon	toasted **fennel seeds**

AN OCEAN TAVERN

1/8 cup	**red wine vinegar**
1/8 cup	chopped **parsley**
1 cup	**extra virgin olive oil**
	salt and **pepper** to taste

Add all ingredients in a food processor except for olive oil. Puree until smooth. Slowly drizzle in olive oil until emulsified. Chill.

This is the dressing we use for our Big Fat Greek Salad .

MAC NUT BRITTLE

4 cups	**sugar**
1/2 pound	**unsalted butter**
12 tablespoons	**corn syrup**
2 2/3 cups	**water**
1 teaspoon	**baking soda**
1 1/2 pounds	**macadamia nut** halves and pieces

In a sheet pan lined with parchment paper and lightly oiled, combine sugar, butter, corn syrup and water. Heat. When color turns to amber, remove from heat. Stir in baking soda and macadamia nuts. Quickly spread the mixture on the parchment paper and spread it out evenly. Allow the brittle to cool and harden. Then break into pieces and store in a covered container.

MAHI MAHI CROQUETTAS

1 cup	cooked **mahi mahi**, chopped and cooled
2	**eggs**
1	**jalapeño**, chopped
1/4 cup	thinly sliced **scallion**
2 tablespoons	chopped **cilantro**
3 tablespoons	diced **piquillo peppers**
1/2	**lemon**, grated zest and juice
	salt and **pepper** to taste
1 teaspoon	**sweet paprika**
1/3 cup	ground **bread crumbs**

Mix all the ingredients in a bowl and form into patties 1/4-inch thick and 2 inches wide. Chill.

Fry for 2 minutes or until golden brown. Drain and serve with lemon and aioli.

Use any fish that has a mild flavor. This is great as a pupu.

AN OCEAN TAVERN

MALA PONZU SAUCE

1/4 cup	**low-salt soy sauce**
1/4 cup	fresh **lemon juice**
1/4 cup	**rice wine vinegar**
1/8 cup	**mirin** (cooking sake)
1	**lemon rind**, 1 x 2 inch, white pith removed

Combine all ingredients except lemon rind in a sauce pan. Bring to a boil. Remove from heat and add lemon rind. Cool and strain through a fine mesh strainer.

We use this sauce mostly for our Fresh Oyster Shooters.

Recipe by Chef Gregory Denton

MALA TARTAR SAUCE

1/4 cup	**mayonnaise**
1/8 cup	**lemon juice**
1/4 cup	chopped **cornichon (gherkin pickle)**
2 teaspoons	**sugar**
2 tablespoons	chopped fresh **parsley**
3 tablespoons	fresh chopped **dill**
	salt and **pepper** to taste

Mix all ingredients together and chill.

MANGO GAZPACHO

4	fresh **tomatoes**, very ripe, core removed
1 cup	**San Marzano tomatoes**, canned
1 cup	fresh **mango pulp**
1/2	**green bell pepper**, chopped and seeded
1/4	**Maui onion**, chopped and peeled
1	**Japanese or hothouse cucumber**, peeled and seeded
1 clove	**garlic** peeled
1 tablespoon	fresh **ginger**, chopped
1 cup	**tomato juice**
1/4 cup	**extra virgin olive oil**
1/8 cup	**red wine vinegar**
1 teaspoon	**fennel seed** toasted
1/2 teaspoon	ground **cinnamon**
1 teaspoon	ground **cumin**
1/2 teaspoon	ground **coriander seeds**
1 teaspoon	**paprika**
1/4 bunch	**fresh mint** *or*
2 tablespoons	**dried mint**
1/4 cup	**bread** soaked in water squeezed dry
	salt and **pepper** to taste

Place above ingredients in a container and puree for 2 to 3 minutes, then strain through a fine sieve. Chill overnight. Garnish the soup with a teaspoon each of the following:

	peeled and seeded diced **cucumber**
	diced fresh **mango**
	diced fresh **tomato**
	diced **Maui onion**
	diced **green pepper**
	chopped **parsley**
and	
1/2 teaspoon	toasted **almonds** or **Mac nuts**
1/4 teaspoon	**extra virgin olive oil**, drizzled

MAPLE DIJON VINAIGRETTE

1	**shallot** minced
3 tablespoons	**Dijon mustard**
3 tablespoons	**sherry vinegar**
1/4 cup	**maple syrup**
1/2 cup	**extra virgin olive oil**
	salt and **pepper** to taste

In a cold bowl add shallots, Dijon, vinegar and maple syrup. Whisk until smooth. Slowly drizzle in olive oil. Adjust with salt and pepper.

We serve this dressing at Mala with our Farmers Salad with Maytag Blue Cheese, and Candied Walnuts.

Recipe by Chef Gregory Denton

AN OCEAN TAVERN

MASCARPONE MOUSSE

8 ounces	**mascarpone cheese**
4 ounces	**heavy cream**
1/4 cup	**powdered sugar**
1 tablespoon	**vanilla extract**
2 ounces	**Frangelico (Hazelnut Liqueur)**

Combine all ingredients in mixing bowl. Start on low, then gradually increase speed. Mix until the mixture starts to tighten up and thicken. Stop mixing and pull out the whisk. When you do this a peak should form. If the peak stays straight and tall then the mixture is ready. Remove from bowl and store in refrigerator. Will keep like this for two days in a cold place. After that the mixture will lose volume and consistency and will need to be re-mixed.

Place into Martini glasses and serve with fresh fruit such as raspberries and mango and sprinkle with toasted nuts.

MAYTAG BLUE CHEESE CREAMED SPINACH

2 pounds	**spinach**, cleaned
2 gallons	**water**, boiling
1 cup	**kosher or sea salt**
	ice to water, 2:1 ratio, as needed
1/4 pound	**unsalted butter**
1/2–3/4 cup	**all purpose flour**

Add salt to water. Blanch the spinach in four different batches. Add spinach to boiling water and remove almost immediately. Cool down in the ice and water mixture. Remove from ice bath as soon as it is cool and squeeze all the water or as much as you can out. Set to the side on paper towel. Keep in refrigerator until ready to serve. In a pot add butter and melt. Add flour a little at a time until the mixture takes on a wet sand consistency. Cook and stir for 3–4 minutes. Remove from heat and let stand for 10 minutes.

Sauce:

1/2 cup	**white wine**
1 pint	**heavy cream**
3 each	**Maytag blue cheese**, walnut sized chunks
1/2 cup	**Parmesan Reggiano**, grated
	kosher or **sea salt**, to taste
3 tablespoons	**black pepper**, ground fresh

Bring the flour and butter mixture back to heat on medium and add white wine. Mix with wooden spoon until all is incorporated then transfer to whisk. This mixture will thicken quickly so have cream ready. When it boils add cream, stir and cook until it comes to a boil again. Add both cheeses and mix well until they melt into sauce. Add small amount of salt and pepper. Remove from heat. It is important not to burn the bottom of the pan as you cannot remove the smell of burnt cream. Bring the cream mixture to room temperature and put in blender. Chop spinach a little. Add to blender, cover and puree. Taste the mixture for seasoning, add if needed. Puree until consistency is smooth and flowing free in blender. Remove and store or serve. To serve, just add to pot and heat or put in ovenproof dish, crumble some cheese and bread crumbs and bake.

Recipe by Chef Gregory Denton

AN OCEAN TAVERN

MEAT MARINADE

5 cloves	**garlic**
1/4 cup	**thyme**, fresh leaves only
1 cup	**olive oil**, pure

Combine the garlic, thyme and 1/2 the oil in a blender. Cover the blender and start to puree the mixture. When the garlic seems to be completely pureed, add the rest of the oil and continue to puree. By adding only 1/2 the oil this will give the garlic a chance to have more contact with the blades of the blender allowing the garlic to be cut very small.

MINT PESTO

1/4 cup	**unsalted almonds**, toasted
1/4 cup	**Parmesan cheese** freshly grated
1/2 cup	**extra virgin olive oil**
1/4 cup	fresh **basil leaves**
1/2 cup	fresh **mint leaves**
1 medium clove	**garlic**
	kosher salt
	freshly ground **coarse black pepper**, optional

Put the almonds, cheese and the olive oil in a food processor and pulse until pureed. Add the basil, mint and garlic and process to a smooth texture. Chill and serve with fresh grilled fish or grilled vegetables.

MOJO VERDE

3 bunches	**cilantro**
3 cloves	fresh **garlic**, chopped
1	**jalapeño**, chopped
2 tablespoons	ground **cumin**
1 teaspoon	**fennel seed**
	small pinch **nutmeg**
	juice of two limes
2 teaspoons	**salt**
4 tablespoons	**olive oil**

Place in a food processor and chop to a smooth paste. Add 1 1/2 cup olive oil while machine is on.

We serve this wonderful flavorful and healthy sauce with grilled Mahi Mahi, but is great on anything.

AN OCEAN TAVERN

OCTOPUS AND EDAMAME SALAD
WITH MISO VINAIGRETTE

1 pound	**octopus**, sliced, cooked
1/2 pound	**Edamame** (Japanese fresh soybeans)
2	**tomatoes**, diced
2 tablespoons	fresh chopped **tarragon**
6	**scallions** sliced, white part only
1 teaspoon	chopped **garlic**
1 teaspoon	chopped **ginger**
1/2 teaspoon	dried **chili pepper**

Blanch beans for 5 seconds in salted boiling water. Shock in ice water. Drain well. Place all above in salad bowl and toss with Miso Vinaigrette.

Miso Vinaigrette

4 tablespoons	**white miso paste**, chilled
1 tablespoon	**Dijon vinaigrette**
1 tablespoon	roasted **sesame oil**
2 tablespoons	**ume vinegar**
1 tablespoon	**light soy sauce**
1/2 cup	**extra virgin olive oil**
1/2 cup	**pure olive oil**
1 tablespoon	fresh chopped **parsley**
	salt and fresh ground **pepper** to taste

AN OCEAN TAVERN

Mix miso Dijon Vinaigrette and sesame oil in a bowl with a whisk. Add ume, soy sauce and emulsify with the olive oils. Season with pepper and salt if needed. Chill.

FRESH AKULE OVEN ROASTED WITH LEMON, GARLIC AND MAUI ONIONS

Hawaiian fish, also known as bigeye scad, *usually salted and dried.*

1	**akule**
1	**Maui onion**
	fresh **garlic**
1 tablespoon	**lemon juice**
2 pieces	preserved **lemon**
	olive oil
	chopped **parsley**

Brush the pan with olive oil and place thin slices of Maui onion on bottom. Place a cleaned akule on top. Score the akule with three small slices and place three slices of fresh garlic in the scores. Pour lemon juice over fish, season with salt and place the preserved lemon on side of fish. Drizzle olive oil on top and cook for 12 to 14 minutes until fish is fork-tender. Sprinkle with chopped parsley.

AN OCEAN TAVERN

PURPLE POTATO PUREE

3 pounds	**Molokai** or **Okinawa potatoes**, peeled cut in quarters
1/2 pound	**unsalted butter**
8 to 10 ounces	**heavy cream**
	kosher salt or **sea salt** to taste
	salt and fresh ground **black pepper** to taste

Put potatoes in large pot and cover with cold water. Add a pinch of salt and bring the water to a boil, then reduce to a simmer. When potatoes are soft enough that you can easily put a knife through them, remove from heat and strain through a colander. Reserve the pot on the side for later use. Place a clean white towel over the top and let sit for 10 minutes.

While the potatoes are under the towel, heat 3/4 of the cream in the pot you cooked the potatoes in. You may need more cream later depending on the potato you are using. Bring to a boil then turn off.

Cube the butter and reserve on the side.

Remove towel from potatoes and place potatoes in a potato ricer and crank potatoes through into the pot that has the heated cream in it. Return pot to stove and heat with light to medium flame. Add butter a little at a time and stir with a wooden spoon until all butter is incorporated. Add salt and pepper to taste. Add more cream if necessary. Turn off heat and serve.

AN OCEAN TAVERN

RAW VEGETABLE SALAD WITH AVOCADO VINAIGRETTE

3 pieces	**frisée** (curly leaves of endive)
8 pieces	**mache** (Lamb's lettuce)
4 pieces	**arugula**
6	**grape tomatoes**, cut in half
1/4 cup	**garbanzos**, whole cooked
1/4 cup	**edamame**, (soybeans in the pod)
1 small	**celery rib**, diced
1 small	**carrot**, peeled diced
1/2 small	**fennel bulb**, diced
6	**sugar snap peas**, diced
1/2	**Japanese cucumber**, diced
1 tablespoon	fresh raw **corn**
1 teaspoon	snipped **chives**
4 oz	**avocado** vinaigrette
	salt and **pepper**
	romaine

Chop the lettuces freshly together except for the romaine and add the freshly diced or sliced ingredients. Add the fresh raw corn, chives, salt and pepper then toss with the vinaigrette. Place on romaine leaf.

AN OCEAN TAVERN

SESAME SEED AND GREEN ONION PANCAKES

1 cup	**Yukon Gold potato puree**, warm
3	**eggs**
3/4 cup	**pastry flour**
1/2–1 cup	**2% milk**
2 tablespoons	**soy sauce**
1 tablespoon	**sesame oil**
2 teaspoons	**baking powder**
1 cup	**green onion**, sliced thin, green part only
1/2 cup	**sesame seeds**, toasted
	sesame oil, as needed
	pure olive oil, as needed

In a bowl mix warmed potato puree and eggs. Add pastry and milk until it is a batter consistency, like a normal pancake batter would be. Add the rest of the ingredients and refrigerate overnight or at least 3 hours. Pull the batter from the refrigerator an hour before use. Heat the olive oil and a drop of the sesame oil in a non-stick pan. Using a spoon or ladle, add batter to heated pan. We like silver dollar size pancakes but you can go with any size you feel comfortable with—just make sure it's easy to flip. Add a little bit of toasted sesame seeds and green onion to top of pancake. Maintain a medium heat. (The heat is very important!) When you start to see bubbles on top of pancake it is time to flip it over. Cook on the other side until the middle of the pancake is firm. Remove, place on plate and repeat.

This takes a little bit of practice. Use a spatula at first and always flip away from you so the hot oil will not burn you. The first batch of pancakes is always the worst so don't give up. Good Luck!

SWEET CHILI VINAIGRETTE

1/4 cup	**sugar**
1/4 cup	**rice wine vinegar**
2 tablespoons	fresh chopped **ginger**
1 tablespoon	fresh chopped **garlic**
2 tablespoons	**sambal** (Southeast Asian chili sauce)
1/2 cup	**water**
1/2 cup	**olive oil**
2 tablespoons	each, fresh chopped **cilantro** and **mint**

In a medium saucepan over medium heat add the sugar, rice wine vinegar, chopped ginger, chopped garlic, sambal and water. Reduce until 1/4 cup of liquid is left. Cool the mixture. Then add olive oil, cilantro and mint. Serve this sauce with any of your favorite grilled meats.

STEAMED CLAMS, GINGER GARLIC
BLACK BEAN SAUCE

3 tablespoons	**olive oil**
2 tablespoons	fresh chopped **ginger**
2 tablespoons	fresh chopped **onion**
2 tablespoons	fresh chopped **garlic**
1 teaspoon	fermented **black beans** well rinsed
	sambal to taste

Sauté the above ingredients over high heat, then add

1 pound	**Manila clams**—triple rinsed (small size if possible)

Sauté for 30 seconds and add

4 ounces	**dry white wine**
2 ounces	**unsalted butter**
2 tablespoons	minced **chives** or **green onions**

Cover and steam clams until shell opens—about one to two minutes. Do not overcook clams. Once they open, remove from heat and add the wine, butter and chives. Pour into bowl and serve with grilled pita or any favorite bread to soak up the essence.

SPICY SUGAR SNAP PEAS

1 teaspoon	chopped **ginger**
1 ounce	**olive oil**
4 ounces	**snap peas**
	dash of **sambal** or to taste
	salt and **pepper**
1 ounce	**water**
1/4 teaspoon	toasted **sesame seeds**

In sauté pan over high heat the olive oil. Add ginger, salt and pepper, snap peas and sambal. Cook for 30 to 45 seconds, then add the water and cook for 10 seconds more. Plate and garnish with toasted sesame seeds.

TOMATO GINGER SAUCE

2 ounces	**olive oil**
2 tablespoons	chopped **ginger**
1 clove	**garlic** sliced thin
	salt and **pepper**
8 ounces	basic **tomato sauce**
2 tablespoons	fresh minced **basil**
2 tablespoons	fresh minced **mint**
	juice of 1/2 lemon

Heat olive oil in medium sauce pan over medium heat. Add the ginger, garlic and salt and pepper. Cook for 30 seconds. Add tomato sauce and cook for ten minutes. Then add the basil, mint and lemon and serve with your favorite grilled fish.

AN OCEAN TAVERN

VOLCANO SPINACH

2 pounds	**spinach**, cleaned
2 gallons	**water**, boiling
1 cup	**kosher** or **sea salt**
	ice to water as needed, 2:1 ratio

Add salt to water. Blanch the spinach in batches of 4. Add the spinach to the boiling water and remove it almost immediately. Cool down in the ice and water mixture. Remove from ice bath as soon as it is cool and squeeze out all the water or as much as you can. Set to the side on paper towel as you blanch and cool each batch. Keep in refrigerator until ready to serve.

2 tablespoons	**unsalted butter**
2 tablespoons	**extra virgin olive oil**
2 cloves	**garlic**, minced
3 tablespoons	**ponzu (see recipe on page 59)**
1/4 cup	**chives**, chopped
1 tablespoon	**sesame seeds**, toasted
	sambal oelek (chili sauce) to taste

Combine butter and olive oil in a sauté pan and melt. Add garlic and cook until butter and garlic starts to brown. Add spinach and mix so garlic stops cooking. Add sambal. The more you use the spicier it will be. I recommend at least 2 teaspoons. Then add the ponzu. Remove from sauté pan and put on plate. Garnish with chopped chives and sesame seeds. Serve with your favorite fish or meat or enjoy it by itself.

AN OCEAN TAVERN

SAMBAL [SAHM-BAHL]

Popular throughout Indonesia, Malaysia and southern India, a sambal is a multipurpose CONDIMENT. Its most basic form is *sambal oelek*, a simple mixture of CHILES, brown sugar and salt. Another popular blend is *sambal bajak* (or *badjak*), which adds CANDLENUTS, garlic, KAFFIR LIME LEAVES, onion, TRASSI, GALANGAL, TAMARIND concentrate and COCONUT MILK. Sambals have a multitude of variations, however, depending on the ingredients added, which can include coconut, meat, seafood or vegetables. Sambals are usually served as an accompaniment to rice and curried dishes, either as a condiment or as a side dish. Sambal oelek and bajak, as well as some variations, can be found in Indonesian and some Chinese markets.

Recipe by Chef Gregory Denton

WOK FRIED OPAKAPAKA WITH SPICY BLACK BEAN SAUCE

1 to 1 1/2 pounds	**opakapaka** or **red snapper**, whole, gilled, scaled and gutted
	flour and **semolina** mix (50% whole wheat flour and 50% semolina flour)
4 cups	**soybean** or **canola oil** for deep frying

AN OCEAN TAVERN

1 tablespoon	**olive oil**
1 teaspoon	**sesame oil**
1 teaspoon	minced **ginger**
1 teaspoon	minced **garlic**
1 teaspoon	minced **onion**
1 teaspoon	**fermented black beans** well rinsed
	sambal to taste
3/4 cup	**dry white wine**
1/2 cup	**unsalted butter**
1/4 cup	**green onions**

Using a small sharp knife score the fish into diamond shapes spacing the cuts about one inch apart. Dredge the fish in the flour, shaking off the excess. Heat the frying oil in a wok until 350 degrees. Meanwhile, heat the olive and sesame oils in a large skillet over high heat. Add ginger, garlic, onion and black beans for one minute. Then add sambal and wine and reduce by half. Stir in butter until creamy, then mix in the green onions. Place whole fish into hot oil and cook on each side for three minutes. Flip and cook for another three minutes. Remove from oil and drain on paper towels. Transfer fish to plate and spoon sauce over fish.

This was one of our most popular dishes we had at Avalon and now its popularity is still ever present at Mala.

YUKON GOLD POTATO PUREE

3 pounds	**Yukon Gold potatoes**, peeled, cut in quarters
1/2 pound	**unsalted butter**
4 ounces	**heavy cream**
	kosher salt or **sea salt** to taste
	black pepper, fresh ground to taste

 Put potatoes in large pot and cover with cold water. Add a pinch of salt and bring the water to a boil, then reduce to a simmer. When potatoes are soft enough that you can easily put a knife through them, remove from heat and strain through a colander (set pot to the side for later use). Place a clean white towel over the top and let sit for 10 minutes. While the potatoes are under the towel, heat the cream in the pot you cooked the potatoes in. Bring to a boil then turn off. Cube the butter and reserve to the side. Remove towel from potatoes, place potatoes in a potato ricer, and crank potatoes through into the pot with the heated cream. Return pot to stove and heat with light to medium flame. Add butter a little at a time and stir with wooden spoon until all butter is incorporated. Add salt and pepper to taste. Turn off heat and serve.

MALA MENUS

MALA OCEAN TAVERN

FIRST COURSE

CRUNCHY CALAMARI
With Aioli & Mojo Verde

SWEET & SPICY CHICKEN WINGS
Pomegranate, Ginger & Chili

SPICY LAMB PITA
With Raita & Grilled Pita

QUARTET OF HUMMUS, RAITA, OLIVES, BABAGANOUSH, FRIED CHICKPEAS & GREEK FETA
Grilled Pita Bread, Flax Seed Lavosh

SUGAR SNAP PEAS
Ginger, Sambal & Sesame Mild, Medium & Spicy

BIG ISLAND ALII MUSHROOMS
Garlic & Parsley a la Plancha

SEARED AHI BRUSCHETTA
Flax Seed Toast, Tomatoes, Edamame Puree

TOMATO SHIITAKE FLATBREAD
Mozzarella Cheese and Basil

GARLIC CHEESE FLATBREAD

HOUSE MADE OLIVES

CHEESE PLATE
Spanish Manchego, Tomme de Savoie,
Fig Almond Cake & Membrillo

SALADS

FARMER'S SALAD - MAPLE DIJON VINAIGRETTE
Maytag Blue Cheese, Kula Greens & Toasted Walnuts

MARK'S CAESAR SALAD
With Grilled Flax Seed Toast & White Anchovies

MY BIG FAT GREEK SALAD
Lemon Tahini Vinaigrette

GADO GADO SALAD (VEGAN)
With Coconut Peanut Sauce

BEET & KULA GOAT CHEESE SALAD
Fennel Vinaigrette
ADD GRILLED FRESH FISH TO ANY SALAD

ENTREES

AVALON SEARED SASHIMI
Shiitake Mushroom Ginger Sauce Mild, Med or Spicy

ONE LB. STEAMED CLAMS
Ginger Garlic Black Bean Sauce, Grilled Pita. Mild or Spicy

BALINESE STIRFRY W/FRESH ISLAND FISH
Snap Peas, Shiitake Mushrooms Organic Brown Rice

PRIME FLAT IRON STEAK ½ LB.
With Caramelized Onions, Ancho Steak Sauce & Frites

TAVERN

AHI BURGER (House Made)
Fresh Ground Ahi with Herbs & Spice, Whole Wheat
Bun, Tartar Sauce, Romaine, Tomato, & Frites

FRESH ISLAND FISH SANDWICH
Whole Wheat Bun, Tartar Sauce, Romaine, Tomato & Frites

ROLLS ROYCE KOBE BEEF CHEESEBURGER
With Smoked Apple Wood Bacon, Caramelized
Onion, Cheddar or Maytag Blue Cheese, Frites
Romaine & Tomato, Whole Wheat Bun

ADULT MAC & CHEESE
Mushroom Cream, Mozzarella, Pecorino & Maytag Blue

DINNER SPECIALS

FIRST COURSE

HOOD CANAL OYSTER SHOOTER
Washington State Oyster, Tobiko, Ponzu & Wasabi

MAHI MAHI CEVICHE
Lime, Cilantro, Kula Greens & House Made Tortilla
Chips

SPICY CURRY POTATO SOUP
Crème Fraiche, Micro Parsley & Lavosh

SEARED TOMBO BRUSCHETTA
Albacore Tuna, Flax Seed Toast, Basil, Tomatoes
Edamame Puree, E.V.O.O & Villa Manodori
Balsamico

MALA OCEAN FLATBREAD
Ahi, Opakapaka, Mahi Mahi, Tombo, Garlic Oil,
Tomatoes, Mozzarella & Basil

ENTREES

MAHI MAHI ALA PLANCHA
Yukon Gold Potato Puree, Green Mojo Verde,
Tomato Relish & Grilled Pita with Romesco

GRILLED OPAKAPAKA FILLET
Potato Puree, Roasted Eggplant, Piquillo Peppers,
Verjus Beurre Blanc & Micro Kale

WHOLE WOK FRIED OPAKAPAKA
Ginger Garlic Black Bean Sauce, Mashed Potatoes
or Rice, Snap Peas, Shiitake Mushrooms Mild, Med or
Spicy

HOISIN GLAZED PORK RIBS
Purple Potatoes, Spicy Edamame Beans, Shiitake
Mushrooms & Coconut Peanut Sauce

ORGANIC CHICKEN PITA SALAD
Mojo Verde, Kula Greens, Raita, Tomatoes, Olives & Feta

GRILLED FILET MIGNON
Potato Puree, Garlic Sautéed Spinach, Alii
Mushrooms, Port Wine Jus & Chives

WE PROUDLY SERVE MAUI KAANAPALI COFFEE

MALA OCEAN TAVERN

MALA'S MARVELOUS MEGA MARTINIS

OUR BIG FAT GREY GOOSE DIRTY MARTINI (France)
Refreshing Grey Goose Vodka & Olive Juice

SENSATIONAL SAKETINI (Netherlands)
Wasabi Vodka/Sake Chilled to Perfection

THE NEXT LEVEL MANGO MARTINI (Sweden)
Level One Vodka, Splash Cointreau & Mango Puree

LUSCIOUS LYCHEE MARTINI (Vietnam)
Kai Lychee Rice Vodka & Soho Lychee Liqueur

RUBYS' FAVORITE GRAPEFRUIT MARTINI (Sweden)
Absolut Ruby Red Vodka & Ruby Red Grapefruit
Juice

POMPUS POMEGRANATE MARTINI (Canada)
Pearl Pomegranate Vodka & Pama Pomegranate
Liqueur

WET & WILD BLUEBERRY MARTINI (Russia)
Stoli Blueberry Vodka & Wild Blueberry Juice

TRAVIS' TROPICAL PASSIONATE MARTINI (Russia)
Stoli Vanilla Vodka, X-rated Passionfruit Liqueur &
Guava Juice

LUMINOUS LEMON DROP MARTINI (Holland)
Ketel One Citroen Vodka, Cointreau & Fresh
Squeezed Lemonade With A Sugar Rim

GODIVA CHOCOLATE MARTINI (Russia)
Stoli Vanilla Vodka, Godiva Chocolate Liqueur &
Baileys Irish Liqueur

KEY LIME PIE MARTINI (Russia)
Stoli Vanilla Vodka, KeKe Key Lime Cream Liquer
with a Sugar Graham Cracker Rim

SWEET AND SPICY GINGER MARTINI (USA)
Yazi Ginger Vodka & Candied Ginger Garnish

PRECIOUS PEAR MARTINI (France)
Grey Goose Pear Vodka and Pear Juice

OUR FAVORITE COCKTAILS

REFRESHING HANDMADE MOJITO
Fresh Mint, Limes, Homemade Lemonade &
Anguilla Pyrat Planters XO Reserve Rum

MALA HANDMADE SANGRIA
Spanish Red Wine, Gran Torres Orange Liqueur
Fresh Limes, Lemons & Oranges

BERRY BOMBER COCKTAIL
Bombay Sapphire Gin, Sweet & Sour & Splash
Chambord

SPUNKY MALA MONKEY
Malibu Coconut Rum, Banana Liqueur, Orange
Juice and Pineapple Juice

FLYING FUZZY RASPBERRY COCKTAIL
Stoli Raspberry Vodka, Peach Schnapps, Cranberry
Juice

MALA'S ORGANIC OCEAN BLUE ON ICE (Maui)
Made on Maui OCEAN Vodka, Soda H20, & Lemon

MANGO MADNESS (Barbados)
Mount Gay Mango Rum, Mango Puree & soda H2O

MALA MANGO DAQUIRI
SUPER STRAWBERRY DAQUIRI
GO BANANAS DAQUIRI
MALA MAI TAI

BEER
ON TAP

BUD LIGHT
BLUE MOON WHEAT ALE
STELLA ARTOIS (from Belgium)
KEOKI SUNSET (from Kauai)

BOTTLES

BUDWEISER
COORS LIGHT
HEINEKEN, CORONA, AMSTEL LIGHT, PACIFICO
MAUI BREWING CO.
   - *Brewed with Aloha right here on Maui!*
- **BIKINI BLONDE LAGER** *Bold, Smooth & Refreshing*
- **BIG SWELL IPA** *Dry-Hopped to Perfection*
- **COCONUT PORTER** *Six Varieties of Malted Barley*

KONA BREWING CO
- **TROPICAL PASSION FRUIT WAILUA WHEAT**

ST PAULI GIRL NON ALCOHOLIC
CHIMAY RED ALE (from Belgium)

SAKE

MOMOKAWA PREMIUM SAKE (Cold)
Diamond - Junmai Ginjo Medium Dry, Oregon 200ml

HAKUSHIKA SAKE (Cold)
Junmai Daigingo, Dry. Nishinomiya, Japan 300 ml

NON ALCOHOLIC DRINKS

MALA PUNCH
Orange, Pineapple, Cranberry and Guava Juices

VIRGIN LAVA FLOW

MANGO SMOOTHIE

STRAWBERRY-BANANA SMOOTHIE

MALA CHOCOLATE MONKEY
Chocolate, Banana, and Ice Cream

O TAHITI WATER
Small
Large

VOSS SPARKLING H2O

NO-JITO
Just as tasty, but alcohol free

ARNOLD PALMER ON THE BEACH
A twist on a favorite - Iced Tea, Fresh Squeezed
Lemonade & a Splash of Guava Juice

REPUBLIC OF TEA
Organic Brewed Teas - Pomegranate Green,
Mango Ceylon Black or Ginger Peach Decaf -
500ml bottles

HENRY WEINHARD'S BOTTLED ROOT BEER

MALA OCEAN TAVERN
AN OCEAN TAVERN

BRUNCH AT MALA
Saturday & Sunday 9am - 3pm

SIMPLE START BREAKFAST
Two Fresh Cooked to Order Eggs, Hash Brown
Potatoes, Grilled Health Bread, Jam, Unsalted Butter

GREAT START BREAKFAST
Two Fresh Cooked to Order Eggs, Mala Hash Browns
Potatoes, Grilled Health Bread, Jam, Unsalted
Butter. Your Choice of the following: Apple Smoked
Bacon, Prosciutto or Lamb Sausage
Or Instead, add Fresh Island Fish of the Day

MALA BENNY
Two Fresh Cooked Eggs on our Health Bread
with Hollandaise & Hash Brown Potatoes
Your Choice of the following:
Lamb Sausage, Prosciutto or Alii Mushrooms
Or Instead, add Fresh Island Fish of the Day

OMELETTE OF THE DAY
Served with Hash Brown Potatoes & Health Bread

TEDDY'S LOCO MOCO
Organic Rice, Kobe Beef Patty, 2 Eggs, Green Onion
& Mushroom Gravy

SERGIO'S KILLER FRENCH TOAST
With Maple Syrup & Fresh Fruit

SERGIO'S HUEVOS RANCHEROS
With Black Beans & Pico de Gallo

CHILAQUILES
Salsa, Corn Tortillas, Two Eggs, Sour Cream & Feta

FRESH FRUIT, YOGURT & MUESLI

FRESH MAUI GOLD PINEAPPLE BOAT

ADDITIONALLY (Served after 11 am)
TOMATO, MOZZARELLA FLATBREAD
Basil & Shiitake Mushrooms

SPICY LAMB PITA
With Raita

ROLLS ROYCE KOBE BEEF CHEESEBURGER
With Smoked Apple Bacon, Caramelized Onion,
Cheddar or Maytag Blue Cheese, Frites

AHI BURGER
Fresh Ground Ahi with Herbs & Spices Whole Wheat
Bun Tomato, Romaine, Tartar Sauce & Frites

FRESH FISH SANDWICH
Whole Wheat Bun, Tartar Sauce
Romaine, Tomato & Frites

MY BIG FAT GREEK SALAD
Lemon Tahini Vinaigrette

ORGANIC CHICKEN CAESAR SALAD
With Grilled Pita

SUGAR SNAP PEAS
Ginger, Sambal, Sesame

BEVERAGES:
Mojito
Bloody Mary
Mimosa
Orange, Guava or Pineapple Juice
Kaanapali Coffee- Regular or Decaf
Hot Tea (Organic)

MALA OCEAN TAVERN
AN OCEAN TAVERN

DESSERTS

CARAMEL MIRANDA
Mark's Signature Dish
A Melted Dark Chocolate and Carmel Sauce
Covered Plate with Layered and Broiled Island Fruit,
Raspberries, Maui Gold Pineapple, Baby Coconuts
& Vanilla Macadamia Nut Brittle Ice Cream

FLOURLESS CHOCOLATE TORTE SOUFFLE
Vanilla Macadamia Nut Brittle Ice Cream,
Carmel Sauce & Whipped Cream

"WEST MAUI DIET" MAUI GOLD PINEAPPLE
Served with 20 Year Old Balsamic Vinegar

VANILLA MACADAMIA NUT BRITTLE ICE CREAM
House Made Carmel Sauce & Coquitos

ROSELANI DRAGON FRUIT SORBET
Fresh Kona Dragon Fruit & Fresh Berries

SPECIAL DESSERT OF THE DAY
PLEASE ASK YOUR SERVER

AFTER DINNER DRINKS

COFFEE DRINKS
CHIP SHOT (Tuaca, Baileys & Coffee)
MINT CHOCOLATE CHIP SHOT
w/Baileys Mint Chocolate Irish Cream
BAILEYS & COFFEE
STARBUCKS CREAM LIQUEUR & COFFEE
KEOKI COFFEE (Brandy, Kahlua & Coffee)
MEXICAN COFFEE
(Tequila, Kahlua, & Coffee

COGNAC
HENNESSEY VS
REMY MARTIN VSOP
MARTELL CORDON BLEU

PORT - DESSERT WINES
TAYLOR FLADGATE RUBY
PX - PEDRO XIMENEZ Spain 1971
DOW 10 YEAR TAWNY

LIQUEUR
AMARETTO DISARONNO
BAILEYS IRISH CREAM
BAILEYS MINT CHOCOLATE LIQUEUR
FRANGELICO
GODIVA CHOCOLATE
GRAND MARNIER
GRAPPA
JAGERMEISTER
KAHLUA
LIMONCELLO
OUZO
SAMBUCA
TUACA

SCOTCH
GLENLIVET
OBAN 14yr.
MACALLAN 12yr.
MACALLAN 18yr.

www.malaoceantavern.com
www.mauitacos.com
www.pennepastacafe.com

82

MALA OCEAN TAVERN

AN OCEAN TAVERN

HAPPY HOUR
3pm - 4:30pm daily

SPECIALTY COCKTAILS

MOJITO
SANGRIA
WELL LEMONDROP
WELL COSMOPOLITAN
WELL MARGARITA
WELL MAI TAI

$2 OFF OUR FAVORITE WINES
MANYANA TEMPRANILLO-*Great Value!*
FAT BASTARD CHARDONNAY

$1 OFF ALL DRAFT BEERS
BUD LIGHT
BLUE MOON HEFEWEIZEN
STELLA ARTOIS
KEOKI SUNSET

$1 OFF WELL DRINKS
$2 OFF FOOD FAVORITES

FLATBREAD
Grape Tomato, Mozzarella, Basil & Shiitake
Mushroom

CRUNCHY CALAMARI
With Aioli

SWEET & SPICY CHICKEN WINGS
Pomegranate, Ginger & Chili

QUARTET OF HUMMUS,
BABGANOUSH, FRIED CHICKPEAS & FETA
With Pita Bread & Raita

FARMERS SALAD with E.V.O.O.
Maytag Blue Cheese, Kula Greens & Grape
Tomato

ROLLS ROYCE KOBE BEEF
CHEESEBURGER
With Smoked Applewood Bacon, Caramelized
Onion Cheddar or Blue Cheese On a Whole
Wheat Bun. Served with Frites.

AHI BURGER   (House Made)
On Whole Wheat Bun with Tartar Sauce,
Romaine, Tomato & Frites

FRESH ISLAND FISH SANDWICH
On Whole Wheat Bun with Tartar Sauce,
Romaine, Tomato & Frites

MARK'S CAESAR SALAD
With Grilled Pita & White Anchovies

BEET & KULA GOAT CHEESE SALAD
Fennel Vinaigrette

"MY" BIG FAT GREEK SALAD
Lemon Tahini Vinaigrette

SPICY LAMB PITA
With Raita & Grilled Pita

GADO GADO SALAD (VEGAN)
With Coconut Peanut Sauce

ABOUT OUR CHEFS

Mark Ellman

Founder/Executive Chef/Owner/Madman, Maui Tacos, Penne Pasta Café, Mala Ocean Tavern

Chef Mark Ellman not only created Maui-Mex cuisine, he is one of the original members of the Hawaii Regional Cuisine (HRC) movement. His "Pacific Rim" recipes are featured in *The New Cuisine of Hawaii*, along with a dozen of his fellow HRC chef friends including Peter Merriman, Roy Yamaguchi, Alan Wong, Beverly Gannon and Sam Choy.

Mark and his wife Judy opened their dream restaurant Avalon in Lahaina in the late 1980s. Although Avalon set the standard for Maui's dining scene for nearly a decade, Mark sold that restaurant in 1993 to concentrate on Maui Tacos. Within a few short years,

Mark, Judy and friend Shep Gordon opened eight Maui Tacos on three islands!

"Maui Tacos was created to fill a niche in the beach culture that is Hawaii. It's a place to come in with sand on your feet, just to put some good food in your body…and go back to the waves again."

Yes, it's true that celebrities do hang out with the surfers at Maui Tacos. Before they came to Maui, Mark and Judy owned the Can't Rock & Roll, But Sure Can Cook catering company in Los Angeles. They provided catering on film locations and backstage for celebrity rock groups including The Beach Boys, Neil Diamond and the Moody Blues. Check out the autographed photos at the various Maui Tacos locations.

Today, Mark personally directs the openings of all the new locations. The Maui Tacos franchise was named one of the top fifty restaurant franchises in the United States for 1999 by *Nation's Restaurant News* ("The NRN Fifty: The New Taste Makers"). There are many Maui Tacos restaurants in Hawaii and the mainland including California, Minnesota, Texas, New Jersey, New York, Utah and Idaho.

Mark is a frequent guest chef on national (and international) television shows including Emeril Live and The Today Show. Mark and Judy live (in that lovely house on the beach) in Lahaina, Maui.

Mark and his wife Judy are up to their elbows with ten restaurants and over 150 employees, but would not have it any other way.

Chef Pepe Vega
Director of Operations, Maui Tacos Hawaii
Partner, Penne Pasta Café and Mala Ocean Tavern

Pepe was born in Tepa, Mexico, outside of Guadalajara. His mother, a chef and teacher to him, was a big influence especially since she taught at a cooking institute. Pepe's love for food is exuberant and apparent in everything he does.

Pepe went to Hawaii originally in 1985 and worked for Compadres Mexican Grill for ten years. This is where he learned from his executive chef brother-in-law, Alfonso. Compadres had Pepe traveling to Honolulu, Lahaina, Napa, and Australia.

In 1996, Pepe returned to Hawaii and fell in love with surfing and the island lifestyle. This time he brought his wife Marcella and two children, Dylan and Ivana, and started working for Maui Tacos. Pepe's responsibilities at Maui Tacos include purchasing, recipe and menu development as well as day-to-day operations.

Together with Sergio Perez and Mark Ellman, they opened a small Italian café called Penne Pasta Café where they continue creating home-style food in a quick service atmosphere.

Pepe's involvement in community, church, family and a little surfing keeps him very busy on this little island called Maui.

Sergio Perez and The Bombay Girls
Executive Chef, Maui Tacos Hawaii
Partner, Penne Pasta Café and Mala Ocean Tavern

Executive Chef Sergio Perez was born in Mexico City on May 27, 1966, destined to cook. He has been around the flavors and smells of kitchens, listening to the rat-a-tat-tat of chopping knives of his father's small but very successful Carnitas Café in the heart of Mexico City. Ever since he can remember, his life has always centered around food.

Sergio's father taught him the art of butchering, the art of salsa making, and the importance of pleasing the public. Sergio's passion and desire brought him to California, where he learned more about his passion for food. He worked at the popular Greek-owned restaurant in Lakewood, California, called Acropolis for eight years. From Lakewood came an offer to move to Maui to work with the new Denny's franchise that was being introduced to Maui. Sergio's passions led him from there to working at Avalon Restaurant in Lahaina, Maui, where he jumped into the world of Pacific Rim Cuisine with Chef Mark Ellman, one of the founding members of the Hawaii Regional Cuisine movement.

Sergio, a hard-working family man, worked many jobs on Maui, sometimes two at a time, while studying at night to become a citizen of the United States of America. His devotion to food and his relationship with Mark led him to being named the executive chef of Maui Tacos, which he's been since its beginning in 1993.

Maui Tacos now boasts eight stores in Hawaii and several franchises on the mainland in California, Minnesota, Texas, New Jersey, New York, Utah and Idaho.

Together with Pepe Vega and Mark Ellman, he opened a small Italian café called Penne Pasta Café where they continue to create home-style food in a quick service atmosphere.

Sergio is very active in the community, doing many cooking demonstrations and traveling with the Hawaii Visitors Bureau promoting Hawaii. Sergio's father is still running his taqueria—twenty-five years later. He is very proud of his son, and I know the people of Hawaii are too.

FRIENDS OF MALA

www.pennepastacafe.com
Great Italian café

www.mauitacos.com
Best Maui Mex food—great fish tacos

www.kona-blue.com
Ocean farmed-raised kampachi

www.surfinggoatdairy.com
Fresh Kula goat cheese

www.kaanapalicoffeefarms.com
Coffee/Maui coffee

www.mauipineapple.com
The best Gold Pineapple in the world

www.freshislandfish.com
Great Hawaiian fresh fish

www.mauibrewingco.com/mauibrewingco.htm
Great handcrafted local beer

www.oceanvodka.com/index.html
Premium organic vodka made on Maui

www.mauiwine.com
Maui's only winery in beautiful Ulupalakua

www.hcsugar.com/products.html
Maui sugar company

www.mauicoffeeroasters.com
Our favorite coffee roaster

www.roselani.com
They make our fresh dragonfruit sorbet

www.onofarms.com
Incredible wild organic tropical fruits

www.oldlahainaluau.com
Best luau on Maui

www.makaiinn.net
Great place to stay right down the block from Mala

www.pennysplace.net
Another nice spot near Mala

www.andreasmithgallery.com/main.html
Our favorite person and artist

www.pieroresta.com/about_piero_resta_artist.asp
A masterful person, artist and friend

www.visitmaui.com
Maui Visitors Bureau

www.reneeloux.com
Friend, cookbook author, chef extraordinaire

www.maui.net/~hanaherb
Organic fiddlehead (pohole) and tropical flowers

www.hhfhawaii.com
Gourmet island grown mushrooms

www.mauiarts.org
Our wonderful performing arts center

www.mauifilmfestival.com
Our very special own film festival

www.mauimarathon.com
Our own marathon and Maui Tacos 5K